Initial Sounds Fold-Ups

Published by World Teachers Press

Order Number 2-5057
ISBN 1-885111-71-1

A B C D E F 98 99 00 01

Educational Resources

395 Main Street
Rowley, MA 01969

Foreword

Initial Sounds Fold-Ups are a fun and interesting way of helping students develop a knowledge of the alphabet, letter names and sounds. Picture clues are provided to help identify initial sounds and words.

The activities provided develop and consolidate students' knowledge and can be folded to make an attractive book for future reference or reinforcement.

Contents

4-5 Teacher Information

6	a	ant
7	b	boy
8	c	cake
9	d	deer
10	e	egg
11	f	face
12	g	girl
13	h	hat
14	i	insect
15	j	jam
16	k	king
17	l	ladder
18	m	mouse
19	n	nest
20	o	orange
21	p	pear
22	q	quilt
23	r	rain
24	s	six
25	t	toy
26	u	umpire
27	v	vulture
28	w	watch
29	x	xylophone
30	y	yak
31	z	zip
32	a	apple
33	b	ball
34	c	cat
35	d	dog
36	e	egg
37	f	fish
38	g	girl
39	h	hat
40	i	ice cream
41	j	jam
42	k	king
43	l	lion
44	m	monkey
45	n	nurse
46	o	orange
47	p	present
48	q	queen
49	r	run
50	s	swan
51	t	tiger
52	u	umbrella
53	v	volcano
54	w	water
55	x	xylophone
56	y	yacht
57	z	zebra

Teacher Information

Introduction

The teaching of initial sounds has long been recognized as an important component in the early development of the English language. Children, in their early developmental stages, rely heavily on the initial sounds in their writing. This book looks at introducing and consolidating initial sounds through fold-up books which children love. The activities contained within each fold-up are the product of many years of practice and application by the author and represent a wealth of experience.

What are initial sounds?

Initial sounds are single letters that make a single sound at the beginning of a word.

It is important to teach the letters in context rather than independently. It is suggested that prior to completing the initial sound fold-up, children are directed to recognize the letter on its own and at the beginning of various words. Children can brainstorm words which begin with the particular letter.

As an extension, children can hunt for words beginning with the initial letter and create a class dictionary of words found.

Development

It is recommended that initial sounds are introduced in order of the most commonly used. A suggested order would be: s, t, b, a, f, c, e, r, o, d, i, h, m, g, n, w, l, p, j, u, q, k, v, x, y and z.

It is also important initially to ensure children learn letter names, not sounds. Letter names remain constant, while letter sounds vary depending on the word. Once children are familiar and confident with letter names, then it is time to introduce the letter sounds.

It is a good idea to ensure there are plenty of charts displaying these letters and words that begin with each letter. Immersion in words and environmental print is the best source for learning. Select words that are familiar to the children and create class books to display them in a meaningful manner.

Teacher Information

The following is a development plan using one of the pages in the book. It is an example of how the activities in this book could be introduced, developed and extended.

Introducing Work

Introduce the children to the initial sound 'a' giving some examples of words which explain this initial sound. Encourage searching, discussion and brainstorming in which children are required to offer other words which may have this initial sound.

Development

1. Children fold along the dotted lines to make a book.

4. (a) Read each word and discuss what it is.
   (b) Children match the appropriate pictures for each word.
   (c) Circle the 'a' sound in each word.

5. (a) Child decides on an 'a' word to fit the sentence. Teacher records each child's 'a' word in the space provided and has the opportunity to gauge individual student's understanding.
   (b) Children complete the picture to match the sentence.

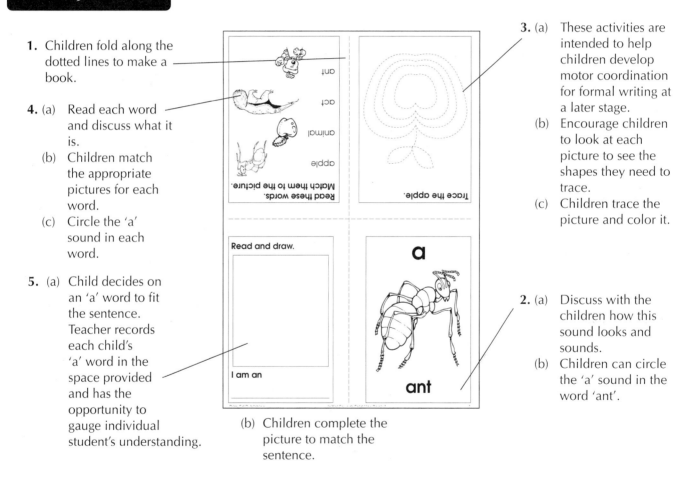

3. (a) These activities are intended to help children develop motor coordination for formal writing at a later stage.
   (b) Encourage children to look at each picture to see the shapes they need to trace.
   (c) Children trace the picture and color it.

2. (a) Discuss with the children how this sound looks and sounds.
   (b) Children can circle the 'a' sound in the word 'ant'.

Extension

Once children complete the initial sounds booklet, they may be encouraged to use the 'a' words in their own writing.
The fold-a-book can also be used as a home reader to reinforce the initial sounds studied in class.

Read these words.
Match them to the pictures.

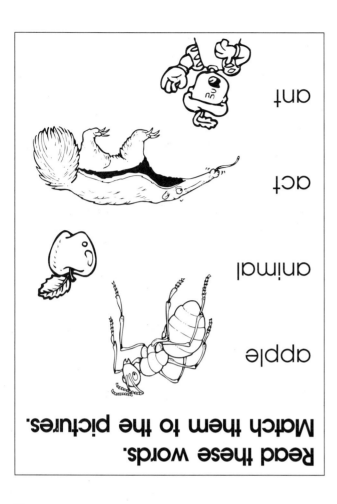

apple

animal

act

ant

Trace the apple.

Read and draw.

I am an

_____

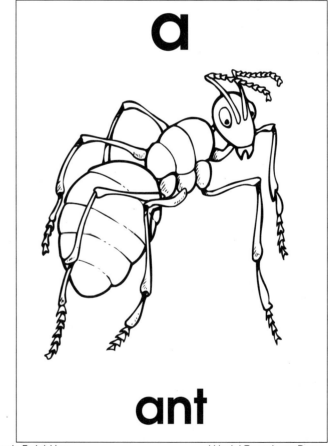

a

ant

Initial Sounds Fold-Ups World Teachers Press

Read these words.
Match them to the pictures.

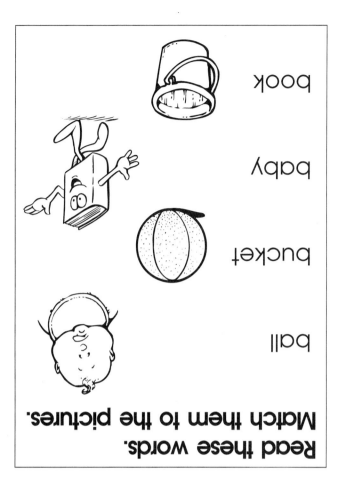

ball

bucket

baby

book

Trace the butterfly.

Read and draw.

I am a

_____

b

boy

Read these words.
Match them to the pictures.

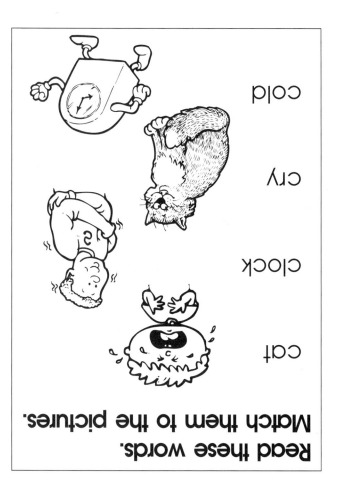

cold

cry

clock

cat

Trace the cat.

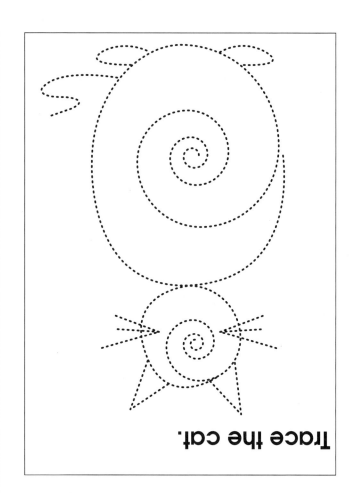

Read and draw.

I am a

_____

c

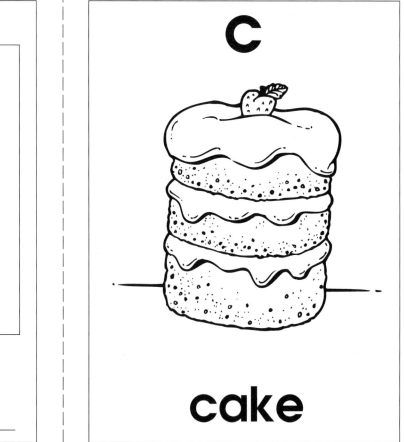

cake

Initial Sounds Fold-Ups World Teachers Press

Read these words.
Match them to the pictures.

dog

dirty

drink

draw

Trace the dog.

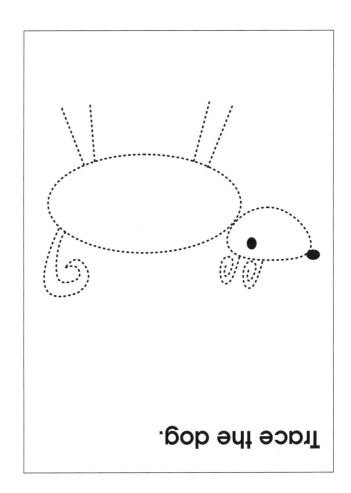

Read and draw.

I am a

_____

d

deer

Read these words.
Match them to the pictures.

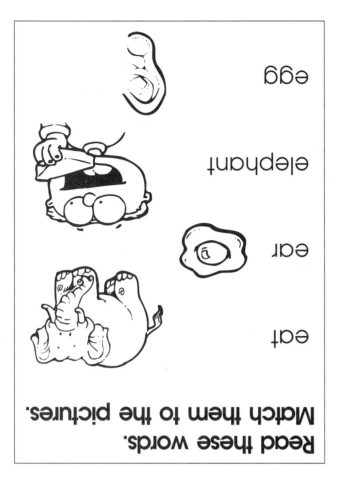

egg

elephant

ear

eat

Trace the elephant.

Read and draw.

I am an

_____

e

egg

Initial Sounds Fold-Ups World Teachers Press

Read these words.
Match them to the pictures.

fish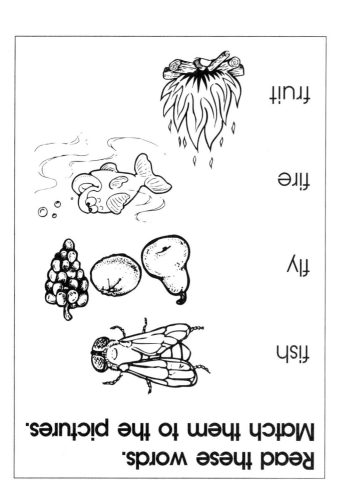

fly

fire

fruit

Trace the fish.

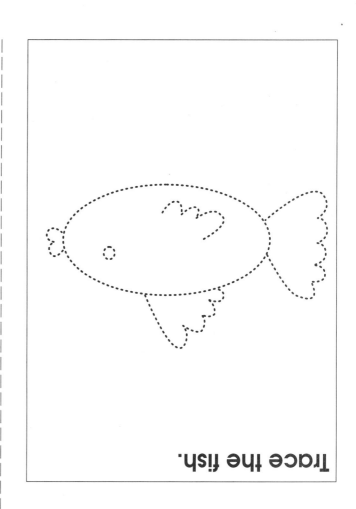

Read and draw.

I am a

_____

f

face

Initial Sounds Fold-Ups

Read these words.
Match them to the pictures.

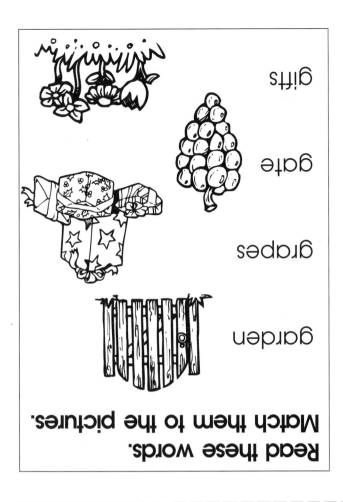

garden

grapes

gate

gifts

Trace the grapes.

Read and draw.

I am a

_____

g

girl

Initial Sounds Fold-Ups   World Teachers Press

Read these words.
Match them to the pictures.

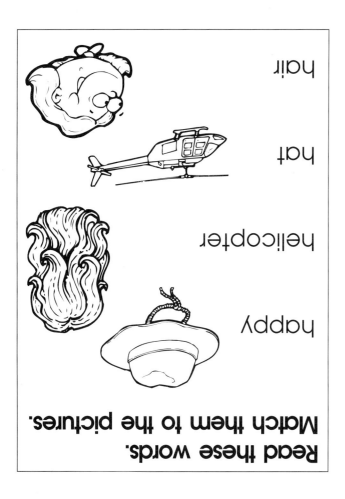

happy

helicopter

hat

hair

Trace the house.

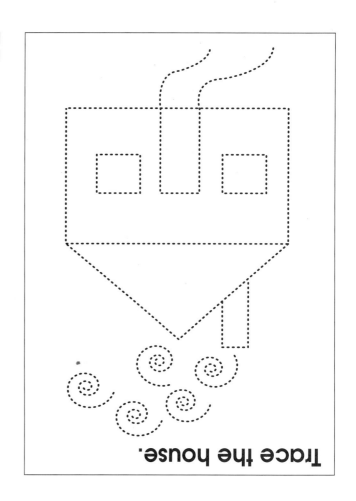

Read and draw.

I am a

_____

h

hat

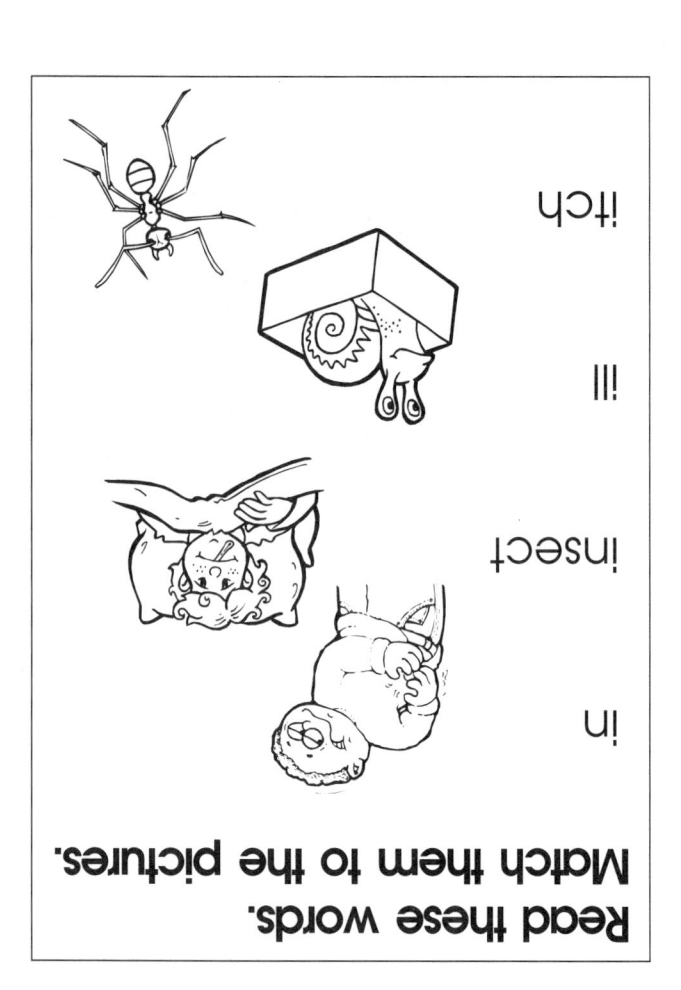

Read these words.
Match them to the pictures.

in

insect

ill

itch

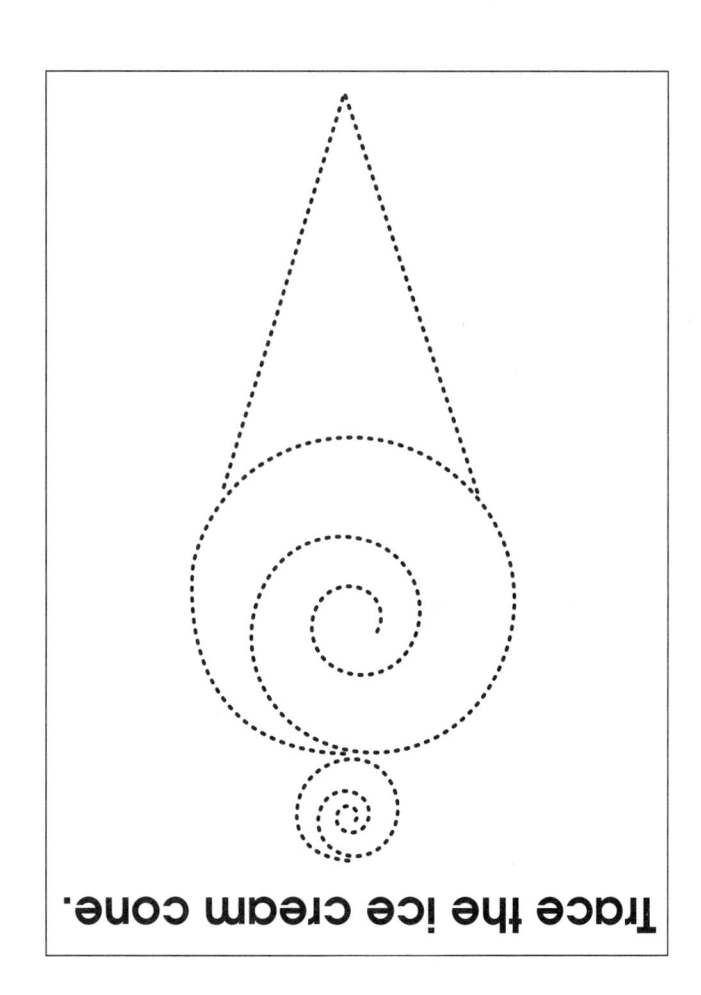

Trace the ice cream cone.

Read and draw.

I am an

_____

i

insect

Initial Sounds Fold-Ups   World Teachers Press

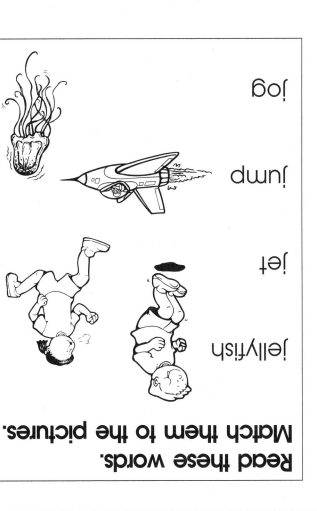

Read these words.
Match them to the pictures.

jog

jump

jet

jellyfish

Trace the jellyfish.

Read and draw.

I am a

_____

j

jam

Read these words.
Match them to the pictures.

Read these words.
Match them to the pictures.

kick

koala

kitten

kiss

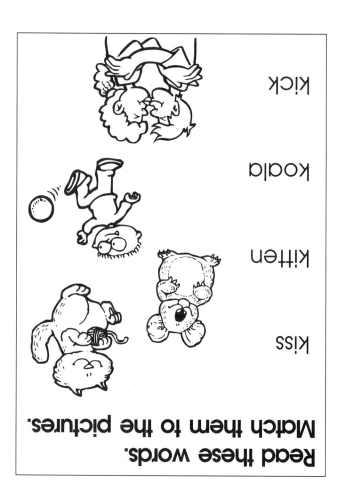

Trace the kite.

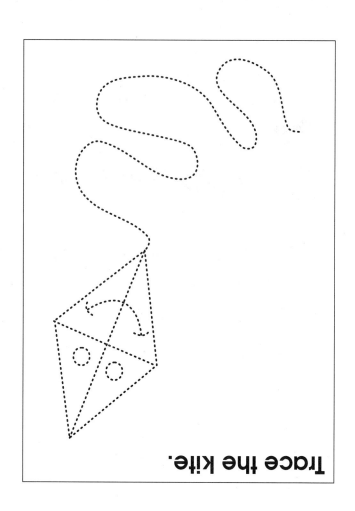

Read and draw.

I am a

_____

k

king

Initial Sounds Fold-Ups

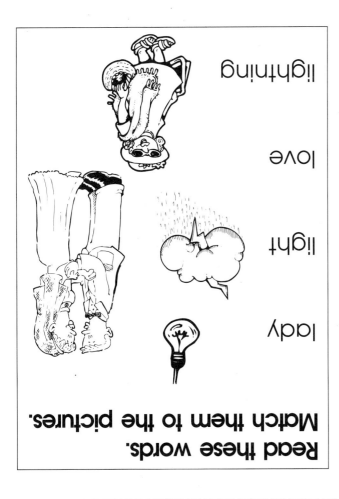

Read these words.
Match them to the pictures.

lady

light

love

lightning

Trace the lion.

Read and draw.

I am a

l

ladder

Read these words.
Match them to the pictures.

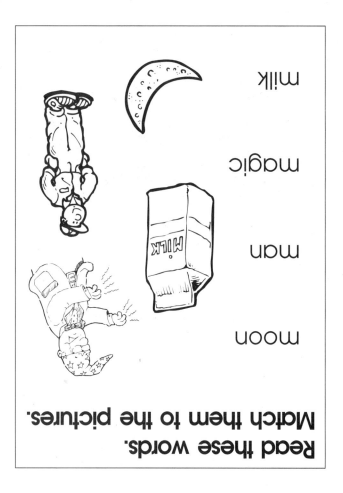

moon

man

magic

milk

Trace the monkey.

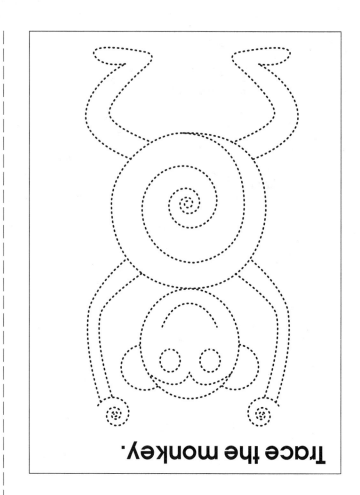

Read and draw.

I am a

_____

m

mouse

Initial Sounds Fold-Ups World Teachers Press

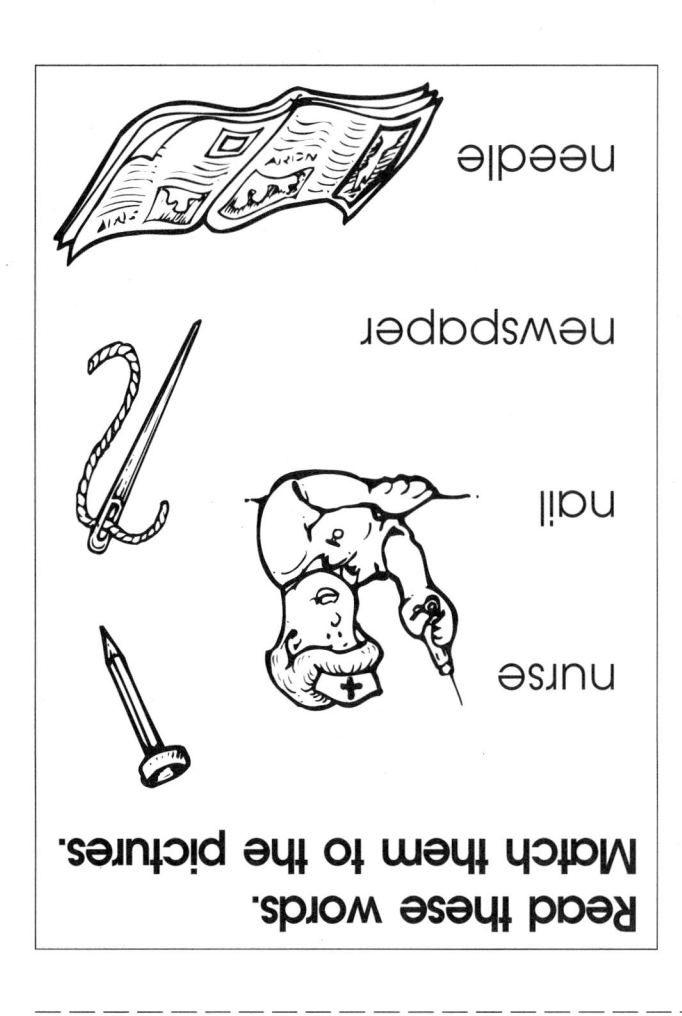

Read these words.
Match them to the pictures.

newspaper

nail

nurse

needle

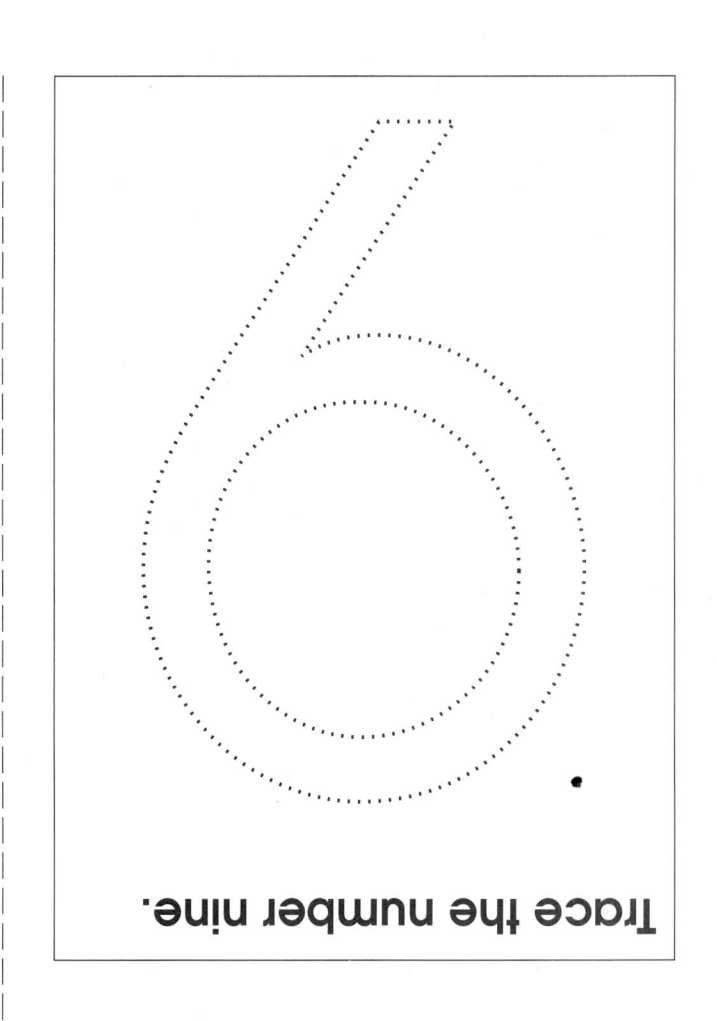

Trace the number nine.

Read and draw.

I am a

_____

n

nest

Read these words.
Match them to the pictures.

overalls

octopus

oil

owl

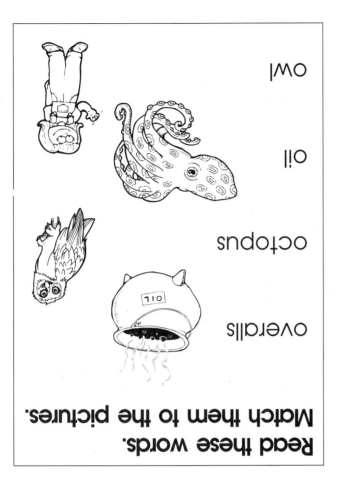

Trace the octopus.

Read and draw.

I am a

I am an

_____

O o

orange

Read these words.
Match them to the pictures.

present

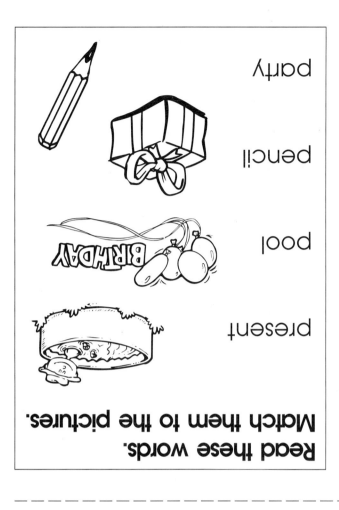

pool

party

pencil

Trace the pig.

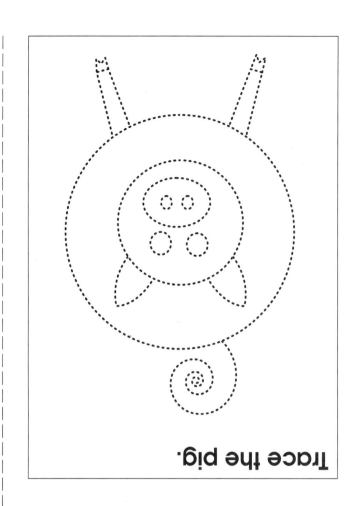

Read and draw.

I am a

_____

pear

p

Initial Sounds Fold-Ups

quill

quail

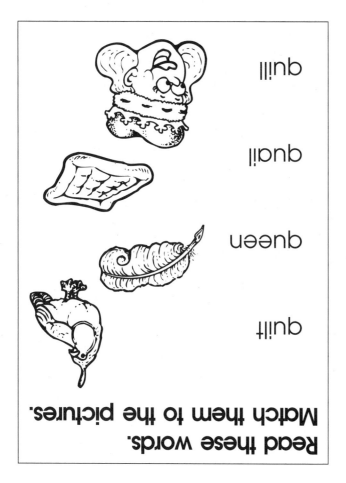

queen

quilt

Trace the queen.

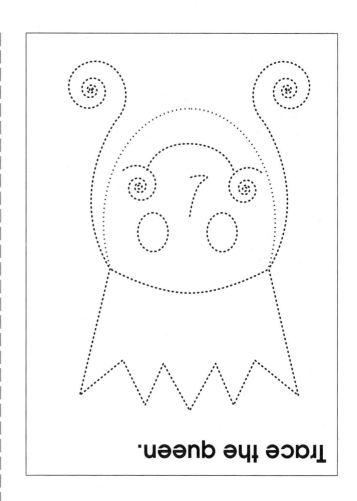

Read and draw.

I am a

_____

q

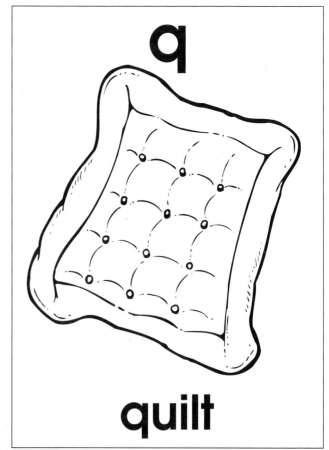

quilt

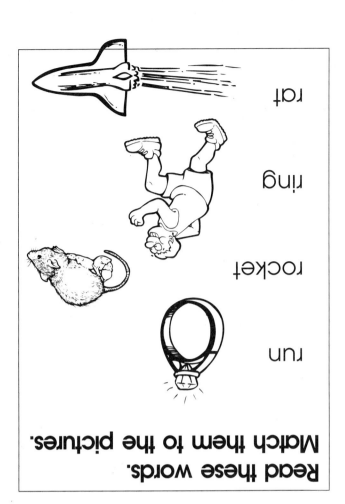

Read these words.
Match them to the pictures.

run

rocket

ring

rat

Trace the rabbit.

Read and draw.

I am a

_____

r

rain

Read these words.
Match them to the pictures.

swim

six

swan

snail

Trace the snake.

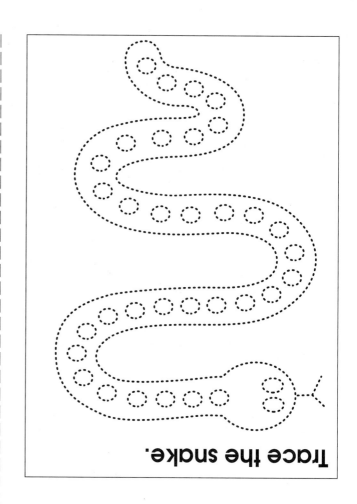

Read and draw.

I am a

_____

S

six

Read these words.
Match them to the pictures.

taxi

television

tiger

ten

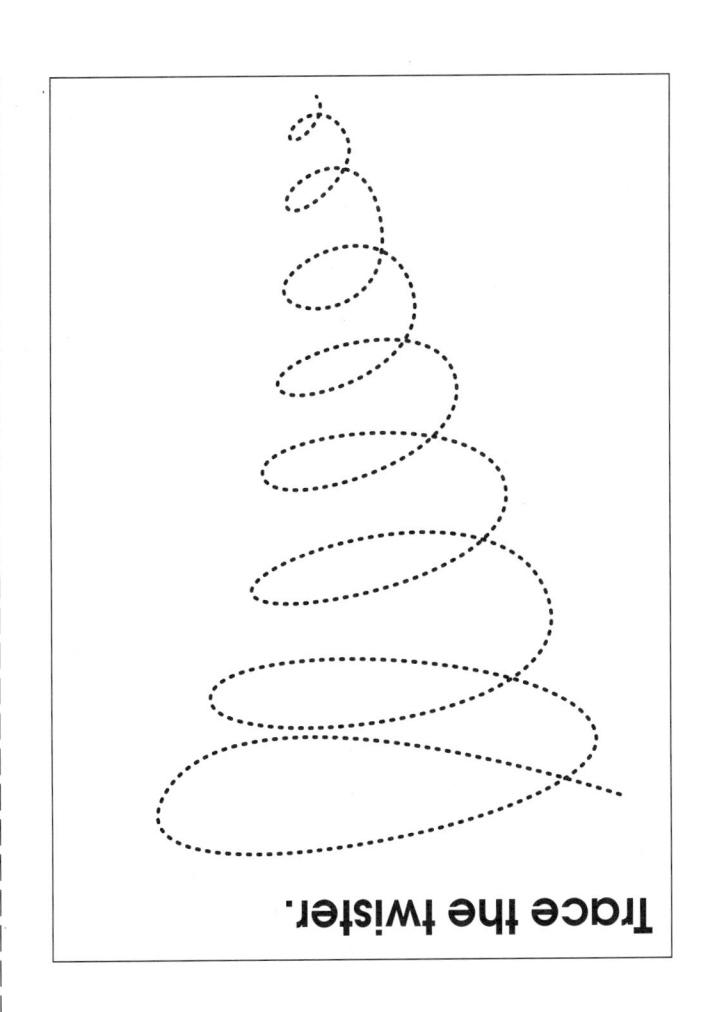

Trace the twister.

Read and draw.

I am a

_____

toy

Read these words.
Match them to the pictures.

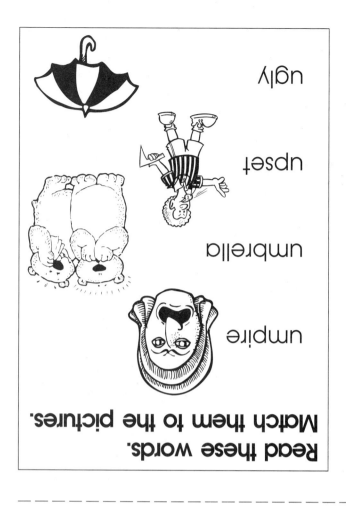

ugly

upset

umbrella

umpire

Trace the umbrella.

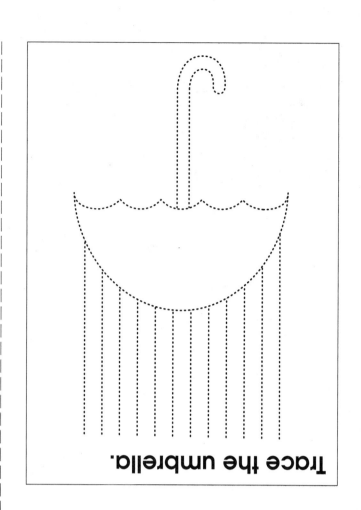

Read and draw.

I am an

_____

u

umpire

Initial Sounds Fold-Ups   World Teachers Press

Read these words.
Match them to the pictures.

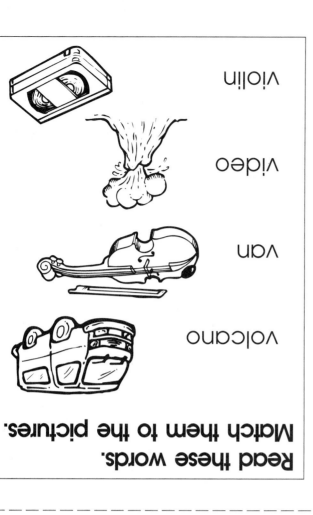

volcano

van

video

violin

Trace the vase.

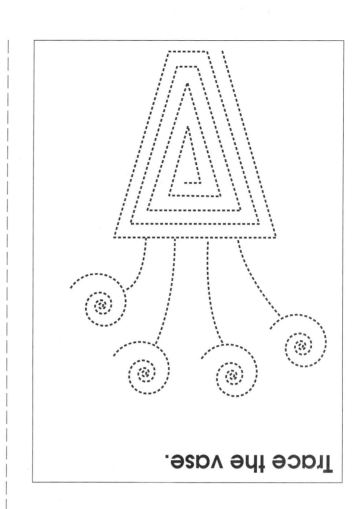

Read and draw.

I am a

_____

v

vulture

Read these words.
Match them to the pictures.

water

walk

warm

window

Trace the whale.

Read and draw.

I am a

_____

W

watch

Initial Sounds Fold-Ups World Teachers Press

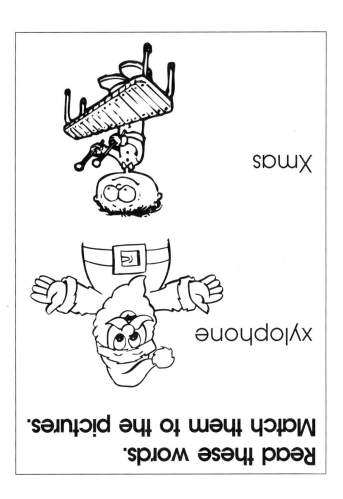

Read these words.
Match them to the pictures.

Xmas

xylophone

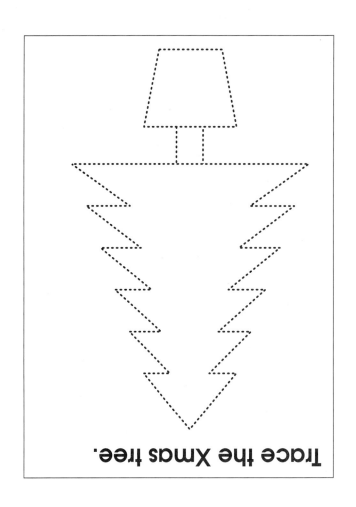

Trace the Xmas tree.

Read and draw.

I am a

_____

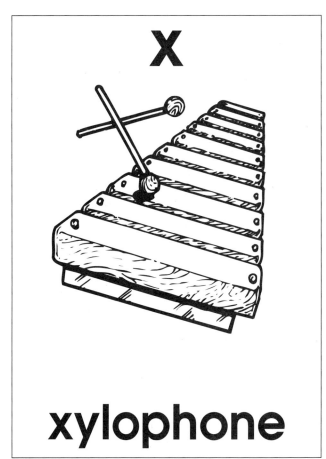

X

xylophone

Read these words.
Match them to the pictures.

yoyo

yogurt

yacht

yawn

Trace the yoyo.

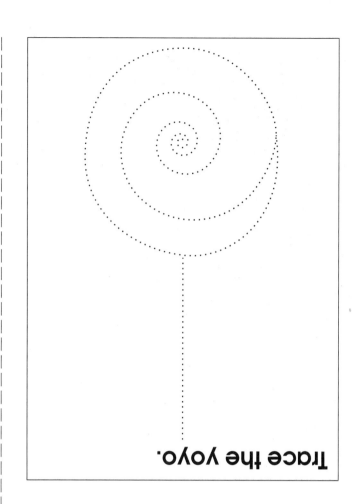

Read and draw.

I am a

_____

y

yak

Initial Sounds Fold-Ups   World Teachers Press

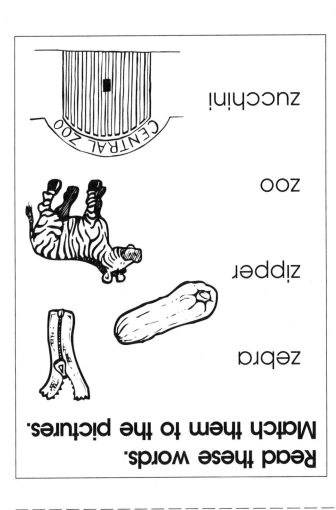

zucchini

zoo

zipper

zebra

Read these words.
Match them to the pictures.

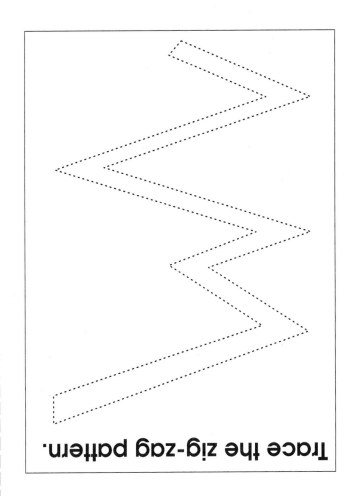

Trace the zig-zag pattern.

Read and draw.

I am a

_____

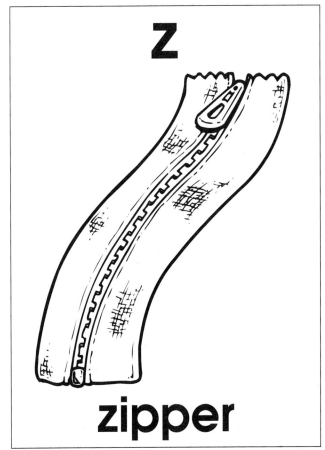

z

zipper

Draw pictures for these words.

animal

ant

Copy these words.

air _____
above _____
are _____
and _____
animal _____
ant _____
after _____

Find the 'a' words.

A	F	T	E	R	A	A
I	A	L	T	H	Z	N
A	N	D	B	K	N	T
O	E				B	C
A	C				D	U
I	P				R	G
R	D				S	V
Q	J	F	X	A	R	E
Y	A	B	O	V	E	M
A	N	I	M	A	L	W

a

apple

Copy these words.

bee

baby

bath

book

boy

big

back

Unjumble the 'b' words.

ybba

atbh

kobo

Draw a boy with a bee.

b

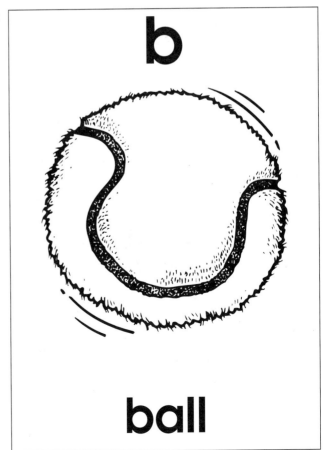

ball

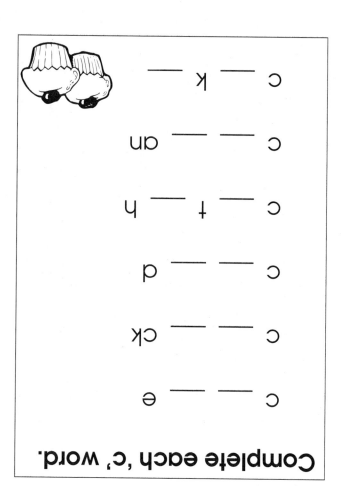

Complete each 'c' word.

c — k

c — an

c — t — h

c — p

c — ck

c — e

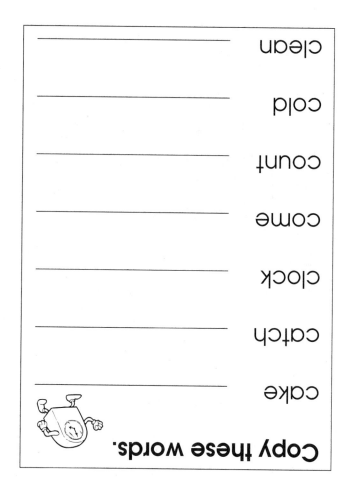

Copy these words.

cake _____

catch _____

clock _____

come _____

count _____

cold _____

clean _____

Find and color the 'c' words.

calclocknmdacatchlcla cleanmamcscoldf pcldfcakemadswoacco untmaclktcomepo

c

cat

Initial Sounds Fold-Ups World Teachers Press

Match the 'd' words to their meanings.

dark • • not clean

door • • opposite to shallow

dirty • • opposite to light

deep • • comes after the night

day • • something you open

Copy these words.

dark _____

day _____

drink _____

door _____

dirty _____

deep _____

drive _____

Circle the 'd' words in the sentence. Draw a picture of the sentence.
The door was very dirty.

---

d

dog

Match the 'e' words to their pictures.

Easter

ear

elephant

eye

Copy these words.

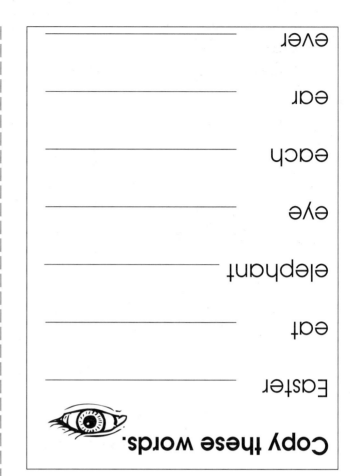

Easter _____

eat _____

elephant _____

eye _____

each _____

ear _____

ever _____

Color the correct answer.

Elephants are small.
Yes   No

You eat rocks.   Yes   No

You have two eyes.
Yes   No

You hear with your ears.
Yes   No

An 'each' is a fruit.
Yes   No

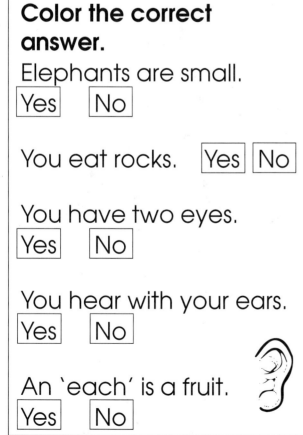

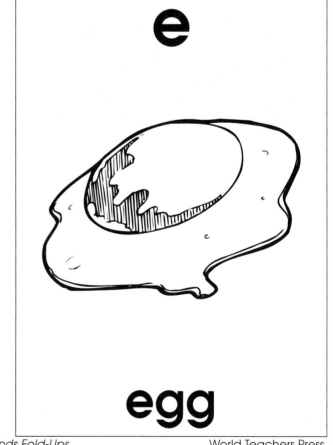

e

egg

Initial Sounds Fold-Ups   World Teachers Press

Complete the 'f' words.

ace   f   ew

ull   eel   ruit

Copy these words.

face

find

full

fruit

feel

fast

few

Complete the puzzle.

fast

feel

face

full

				s	t
		c	e		
			e		
	u				

---

f

fish

Draw pictures for these words.

gate

garden

Copy these words.

garden

gate

glass

game

glad

grow

good

Find the 'g' words.

G	A	T	E	A	B	G
Q	U	I	V	P	C	O
G	A	M	E	T	H	O
S	J				G	D
O	G				G	R
F	V				N	G
D	E				G	R
G	L	A	S	S	M	O
L	G	L	A	D	K	W
G	A	R	D	E	N	G

g

girl

Unjumble these 'h' words.

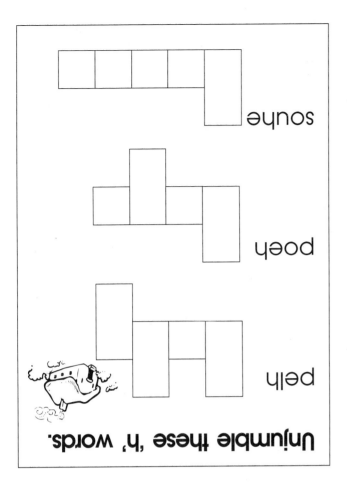

pelh

poeh

souhe

Copy these words.

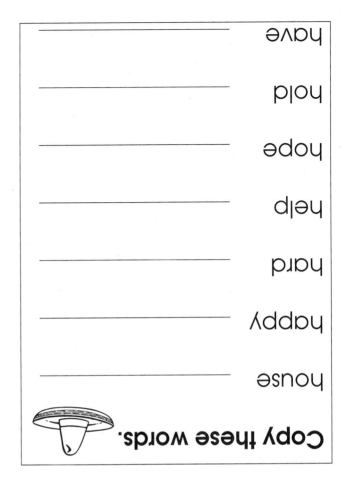

house

happy

hard

help

hope

hold

have

Draw a happy cat near a house.

h

house

Complete each 'i' word.

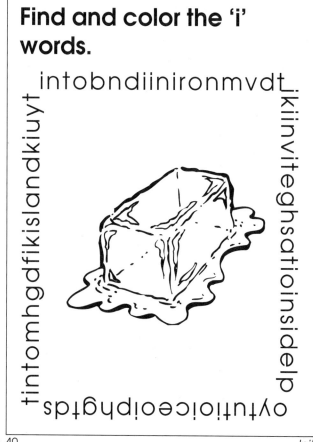

i ___ o

i ___ id

i ___

i ___ te

i ___ a ___ p

i ___ on

Copy these words.

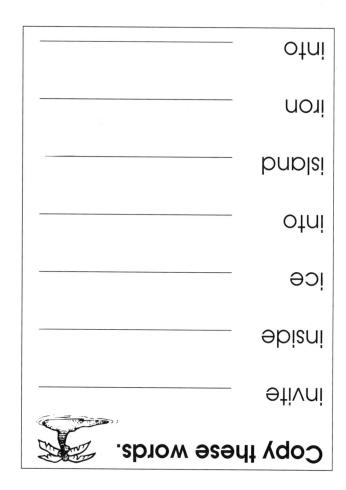

invite _____

inside _____

ice _____

into _____

island _____

iron _____

into _____

Find and color the 'i' words.

intobndiinironmvdt

tintomhgdfikislandkiuyt

kiinviteghsatioinsidelp

oytuttioiceoiphgtfs

i

ice cream

Match the 'j' words to their meanings.

jar • • a frog does this

joke • • part of your face

jump • • something to be done

jaw • • something funny

job • • a glass container

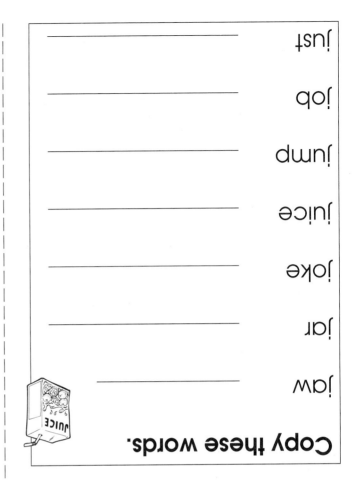

Copy these words.

jaw _____

jar _____

joke _____

juice _____

jump _____

job _____

just _____

Circle the 'j' words in the sentence. Draw a picture of the sentence.

There was just a jar of juice on the table.

j

jam

Copy these words.

kite _____
keep _____
key _____
kind _____
kitten _____
kiss _____
kick _____

Match the 'k' words to their pictures.

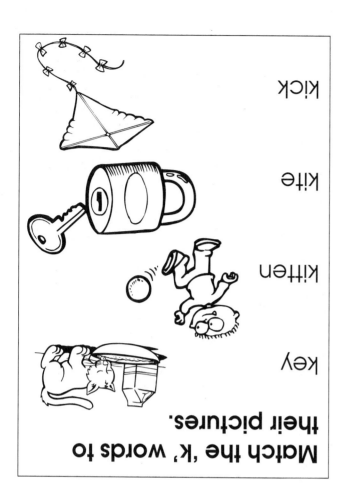

key

kitten

kite

kick

Color the correct answer.

A kite flies.
Yes   No

Kind means to be mean.
Yes   No

A kiss is a type of long snake.
Yes   No

A kitten is a baby cat.
Yes   No

---

k

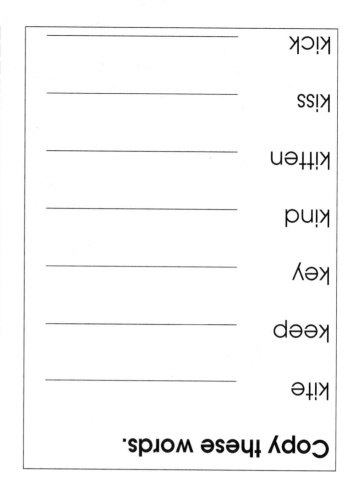

king

Initial Sounds Fold-Ups   World Teachers Press

Complete the 'l' words.

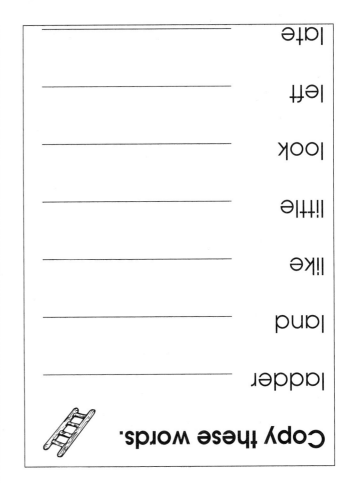

ook   eff   l   ate

ike   adder

Copy these words.

ladder

land

like

little

look

left

late

Complete the puzzle.

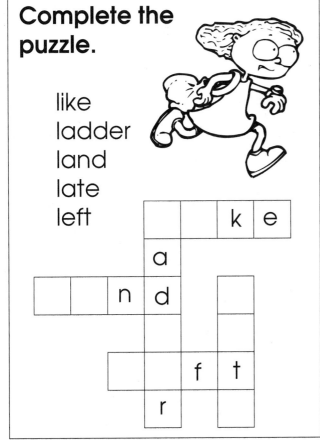

like
ladder
land
late
left

			k	e
		a		
	n	d		
		f	t	
		r		

l

lion

Initial Sounds Fold-Ups

Draw pictures for these words.

moon

man

Copy these words.

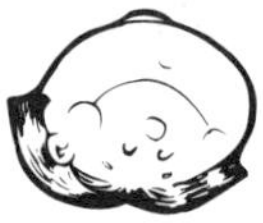

milk ____________

man ____________

moon ____________

make ____________

mine ____________

more ____________

much ____________

Find the 'm' words.

M	A	N	P	F	A	O
I	M	E	M	I	N	E
M	O	O	N	N	V	M
M	H				J	U
D	S				U	C
T	M				M	H
G	K				B	C
M	O	R	E	M	R	Y
M	O	M	M	A	K	E
M	I	L	K	X	L	W

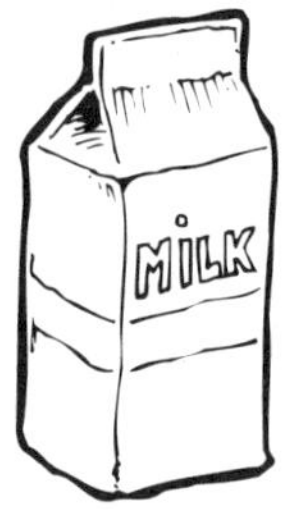

m

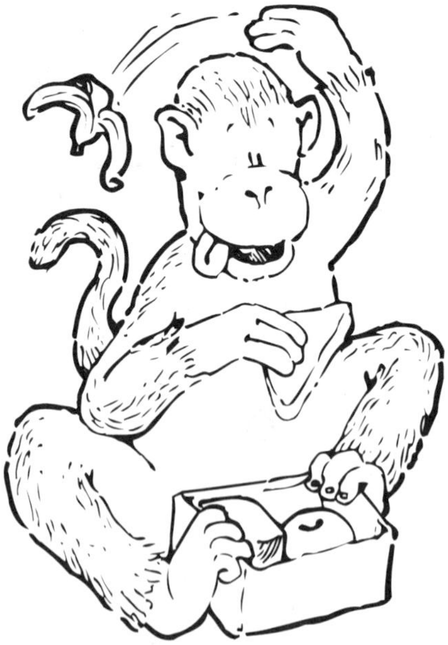

monkey

Unjumble the 'n' words.

tinhg

mane

tens

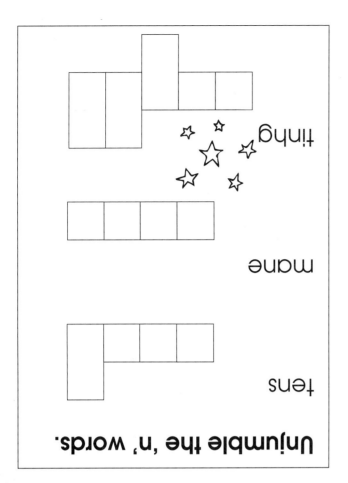

Copy these words.

now _____

night _____

nail _____

name _____

near _____

nose _____

nest _____

Draw a nest near a
house at night.

n

nurse

Initial Sounds Fold-Ups   World Teachers Press

Complete each 'o' word.

o __ r

o __ f

o __ en

o __ r

o __ er

o __ n

Copy these words.

over _____

once _____

other _____

our _____

often _____

off _____

open _____

Find and color the 'o' words.

wuocovernmohtep
aotherbounosoftenmjoi
asopenprtadonuohrour
ktdoncejgsyoftwret

o

orange

p

present

Circle the 'p' words in the sentence. Draw a picture of the sentence.

The pet dog played with the pencil.

Match the 'p' words to their meanings.

pencil •	• you swim in it
pet •	• opposite to pull
pool •	• opposite to push
pull •	• an animal
push •	• you write with it

Copy these words.

pencil ____________

pet ____________

played ____________

pool ____________

push ____________

pull ____________

paper ____________

Complete the 'q' words.

uilt   uiz   q   uite

uack   ueer

_____

_____

_____

_____

_____

Copy these words.

quilt _____

quiz _____

quite _____

quick _____

queer _____

quack _____

question _____

Color the correct answer.

A quilt keeps you warm.
| Yes | | No |

Quick means slow.
| Yes | | No |

Quack is the noise a duck makes.
| Yes | | No |

Question is the opposite to answer.
| Yes | | No |

q

queen

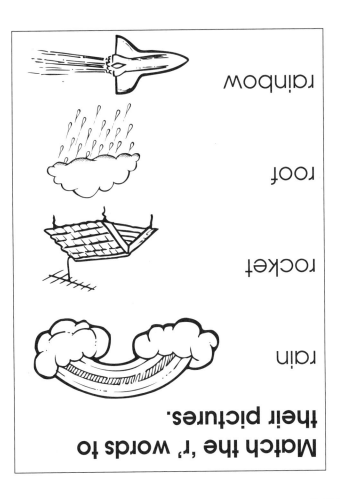

Match the 'r' words to their pictures.

rainbow

roof

rocket

rain

Copy these words.

read _____

room _____

rest _____

rainbow _____

roof _____

rocket _____

rain _____

Complete the puzzle.

read
room
rainbow
rain

	e		d
	a		
			n
o		m	

r

run

Draw pictures for these words.

shoe

star

Copy these words.

star

shoe

street

same

she

school

slow

Find the 's' words.

S	H	E	C	A	B	S
M	F	Q	I	O	E	T
S	S	A	M	E	S	A
L	A				P	R
O	S				D	L
W	N			S	C
J	G			K	S
R	S	C	H	O	O	L
S	T	R	E	E	T	S
S	H	O	E	H	T	B

s

swan

Initial Sounds Fold-Ups World Teachers Press

Unjumble the 't' words.

katt

ntair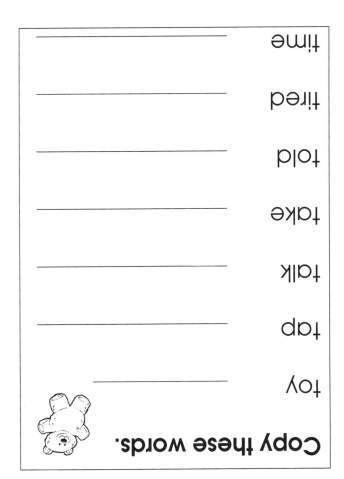

driet

Copy these words.

toy _____

tap _____

talk _____

take _____

told _____

tired _____

time _____

Draw a toy near a table.

t

tiger

Complete each 'u' word.

u _ _ _ et

u _ _ o

u _ _ ss

u _ _ ll

u _ _ u

u _ d _ r

Copy these words.

under _____

upon _____

until _____

unless _____

upset _____

untidy _____

undo _____

Find and color the 'u' words.

mnundokapuhupst

opyteuponwysdundero

iuntidyghaouptgupset

kndounlesspountil

u

umbrella

Match the 'v' words to their meanings.

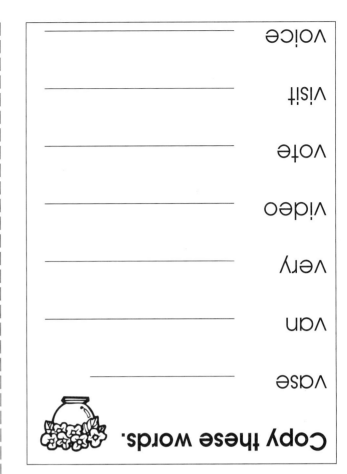

video •   • seen through a television

visit •   • holds flowers

van •   • to go somewhere

vase •   • a type of small truck

Copy these words.

voice _____

visit _____

vote _____

video _____

very _____

van _____

vase _____

Circle the 'v' words in the sentence. Draw a picture of the sentence.

There is a very large vase near a van.

V

volcano

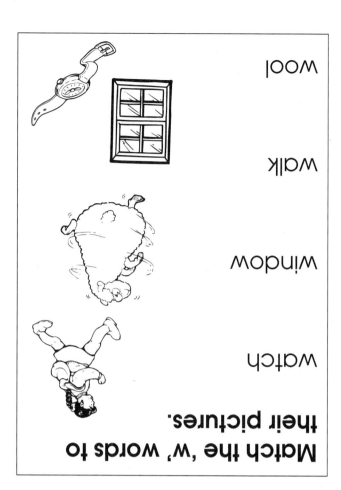

Match the 'w' words to their pictures.

watch

window

walk

wool

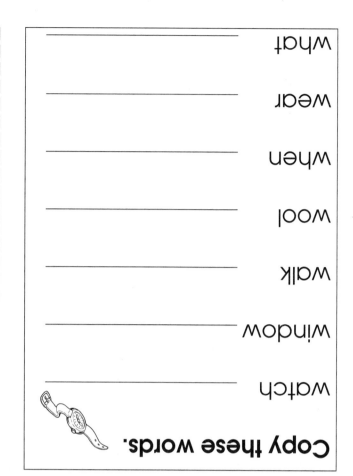

Copy these words.

watch _____

window _____

walk _____

wool _____

when _____

wear _____

what _____

Color the correct answer.

A watch tells the time.
Yes   No

Wool comes from frogs.
Yes   No

A window is made from glass.
Yes   No

A 'wear' is a type of bee.
Yes   No

W

water

Top-right panel (inverted)

Copy these words.

xylophone

X-ray

Xmas

Top-left panel (inverted)

Complete the 'x' words.

ylophone   x   -ray

mas

Bottom-left panel

Unjumble these 'x' words.

y-xar

□ – □ □

eyopxnhol

x   e

amXs

Bottom-right panel

X

xylophone

Draw pictures for these words.

yo-yo

yak

Copy these words.

yo-yo

_____

yak

_____

you

_____

young

_____

yellow

_____

year

_____

yell

_____

Find the 'y' words.

Y	O	U	A	E	F	Y
G	Y	T	H	P	S	A
R	Y	E	A	R	Y	K
M	O				E	Q
B	W				L	L
V	C				L	X
D	X				Y	E
Y	E	L	L	O	W	Y
Y	O	U	N	G	T	K
I	J	Y	Y	O	Y	O

---

y

yacht

Unjumble these 'z' words.

ozo

szet

roze

Copy these words.

zoo

zipper _____

zero _____

zoom _____

zest _____

zone _____

Draw a zebra at the zoo.

z

zebra

Phonics in Context
Activity Phonics

Phonics in Context
Activity Phonics